Riddles and Brain

Teasers for Smart Kids

Over 300 Funny, Difficult and Challenging Riddles,

Brain Teasers and Trick Questions Fun for Family and

Children

DL Digital Entertainment
MADE TO ENTERTAIN

DL Digital Entertainment

errors, omissions, or inaccuracies.

TABLE OF CONTENTS

INTRODUCTION

We would like to personally thank you for taking the time to purchase our book *Riddles and Brain Teasers for Smart Kids*. We've spent countless hours putting together only the best, laugh out loud, challenging and difficult riddles, brain teasers and trick questions for you, the kids and the family to enjoy! You can expect to find in over 300 different riddles, brain teasers and trick questions put into different categories. These categories will consist of: Funny (warm up), Easy Difficulty, Medium Difficulty, Hard Difficulty and Hardest Difficulty in order to make it the most fun experience with the kids, friends and family!

Riddles and Brain Teasers for Smart Kids is very versatile thanks to being available in audio format on Audible.com! Use it on your own before bed, with friends at a get together, with family at the dinner table or camping with relatives; the possibilities with *Riddles and Brain Teasers for Smart Kids* are endless. Be creative and utilize it to its full potential!

WHY RIDDLES?

This ultimate assortment of riddles, brain teasers and trick questions for kids, family and friends will not only challenge you, but it will do so in a fun and interactive way. Riddles have been around since the dawn of time and have many other benefits such as:

-Confidence Boosting: *With so many kids and people in general struggling with self-confidence in our day and age, listening and interacting with these riddles in a safe environment with family and friends gives them the opportunity to comfortably say answers and repeat funny and challenging riddles, giving them the ability to not be afraid to express themselves.*

-Relieve Stress: *Riddles and puzzles like these help in relieving your anger, depression, tension and stress and make you feel light and irritation free. It also improves the mood by reducing anxiety and fear. Laughter increases heart rate and blood pressure, both of which cools down your stress response.*

-Improved Bonding: *Riddles and Brain Teasers for Smart Kids is one of the best ways for friends and family to spend time with each other and build positive, healthy relationships through laughter and participation when listening to the riddles and trying to answer them.*

-Personal Health: *Riddles and brain teasers test our mind and impacts the body in a very positive way. When you start to solve a puzzle, it not only lightens your body but also induces many physical changes in it as well. Not only that, but funny riddles boost up the human immune system by increasing infection fighting antibodies.*

-Reduce Boredom: Having an audiobook such as Riddles and Brain Teasers for Smart Kids gives you the ability to have fun and entertainment on demand. Since we provide it in audiobook form, it gives you the opportunity to utilize it in any situation!

-Develop Humor: Riddles and brain teasers sharpen your sensibilities and tune our capabilities. It improves your personality by bringing out your lighter side. Humor and puzzles also allow people to express their feelings without any hesitation.

Now, that's enough talking. Are you ready to get started with *Riddles and Brain Teasers for Smart Kids.*

Awesome! Let's Begin.

FUNNY RIDDLES AND BRAIN TEASERS (WARM UP!)

Use these funny riddles as a way to warm up for the harder ones coming later on in the book!

1. It has a neck but no head. What is it?

   Answer: A bottle

2. It has one eye but cannot see? What is it?

   Answer: A needle

3. It has four eyes but cannot see? What is it?

   Answer: Mississippi

4. It has hands but cannot clap? What is it?

   Answer: A clock

5. You can catch it, but not throw it? What is it?

   Answer: A cold

6. This travels around the world but stays in one spot?
   What is it?

   Answer: A stamp

7. It gets beaten, and whipped, but never cries? What
   is it?

   Answer: An egg

8. It comes down but never goes up? What is it?

   Answer: Rain

9. It has a hundred limbs, but cannot walk? What is it?

   Answer: A tree

10. You can you serve it, but never eat it? What is it?

    Answer: A tennis ball

11. It has eyes that cannot see, a tongue that cannot taste, and a soul that cannot die. What is it?

    Answer: A shoe

12. This type of dress can never be worn. What is it?

    Answer: An address

13. This bet can never be won. What is it?

    Answer: The alphabet

14. This kind of coat can you put on only when it is wet. What is it?

    Answer: A coat of paint

15. It flies around all day but never goes anywhere? What is it?

    Answer: A flag

16. This goes up and down, but never moves? What is it?

    Answer: A flight of stairs

17. It wears a jacket, but no pants. What is it?

    Answer: A book

18. This can clap without any hands. What is it?

    Answer: Thunder

19. It has a bark, but no bite. What is it?

    Answer: A tree

20. It has a neck but no head, and wears a cap? What is it?

    Answer: A bottle

21. It is easy to get into, but hard to get out of? What is it?

    Answer: Trouble

22. What does a cat have that no other animal has?

    Answer: Kittens

23. What has two heads, four eyes, six legs, and a tail?

    Answer: A cowboy riding his horse

24. What always sleeps with its shoes on?

Answer: A horse

25. What is as big as an elephant, but weighs nothing at all?

    Answer: The shadow of an elephant

26. What fur do we get from a Tiger?

    Answer: As fur away as possible!

27. Why do dragons sleep all day?

    Answer: They like to hunt knights.

28. What can honk without a horn?

    Answer: A goose

29. What has a horn but does not honk?

    Answer: A rhinoceros

30. What is the greatest worldwide use of cowhide?

Answer: To cover cows

31. What two keys can't open any doors?

Answer: A donkey and a monkey

32. A frog jumped into a pot of cream and started treading. He soon felt something solid under his feet and was able to hop out of the pot. What did the frog feel under his feet?

Answer: The frog felt butter under his feet, because he churned the cream and made butter.

33. A horse is on a 24 foot chain and wants an apple that is 26 feet away. How can the horse get to the apple?

Answer: The chain is not attached to anything.

34. I can sizzle like bacon, I am made with an egg, and I have plenty of backbone, but lack a good leg. I peel layers like onions, but still remain whole; I can be long, like a flagpole, yet fit in a hole. What am I?

Answer: A snake

35. Name three days consecutively where none of the seven days of the week appear.

Answer: Yesterday, Today, and Tomorrow

36. Why did the woman wear a helmet at the dinner table?

Answer: Because of her crash diet

37. What do you call a fairy that has not taken a bath?

Answer: Stinker Bell

38. Which word in the dictionary is spelled incorrectly?

Answer: Incorrectly

39. Why are teddy bears never hungry?

    Answer: Because they are always stuffed

40. What did the chewing gum say to the shoe?

    Answer: I am stuck on you

41. Why was the belt arrested?

    Answer: For holding up the pants

42. What do you call a funny book about eggs?

    Answer: Yolk book

43. What is the best cure for dandruff?

    Answer: Baldness

44. What do you call a man who does not have all his fingers on one hand?

Answer: Normal – You have fingers on both hands!

45. What does an invisible man drink at snack time?

    Answer: Evaporated milk

46. What did the beach say when the tide came in?

    Answer: Long time, no sea

47. What did one potato chip say to the other?

    Answer: Shall we go for a dip?

48. Why couldn't the sailors play cards?

    Answer: The captain was standing on the deck

49. What is the best thing to do if a bull charges you?

    Answer: Pay the bull

50. Why can't you play basketball with pigs?

Answer: Because they hog the ball

51. Which football player wears the biggest helmet?

Answer: The one with the biggest head

52. What did the outlaw get when he stole a calendar?

Answer: Twelve months

53. In which month do monkeys play baseball?

Answer: Ape-ril

54. How do rabbits travel?

Answer: By hare plane

55. Have you heard about the restaurant on the moon?

Answer: Great food, but no atmosphere

56. Why didn't the hot dog star in the movies?

    Answer: The roll was not good enough.

57. What is black, white, and pink all over?

    Answer: An embarrassed zebra

58. Suproliglicatiouspenuvaliancia – how do you spell it?

    Answer: I T (it)

59. Why is the Mississippi such an unusual river?

    Answer: Because it has four eyes and it cannot even see!

60. When is a car, not a car?

    Answer: When it turns into a parking lot

EASY DIFFICULTY

1. What bank never has any money?

   Answer: The riverbank

2. Why isn't your nose twelve inches long?

   Answer: Because then it would be a foot.

3. What has many rings, but no fingers?

   Answer: A telephone

4. What are two things you cannot have for breakfast?

   Answer: Lunch and dinner

5. What kind of cup can't hold water?

   Answer: A cupcake

6. Why did the bumble bee put honey under his pillow?

   Answer: He wanted to have sweet dreams.

7. What is the longest word in the dictionary?

   Answer: Smiles, because there is a mile between each "s"

8. Which weighs more, a pound of feathers or a pound of bricks?

   Answer: Neither, they both weigh one pound!

9. Blue lives in the blue house, Mr. Pink lives in the pink house, and Mr. Brown lives in the brown house. Who lives in the white house?

   Answer: The President

10. What goes through towns and over hills but never moves?

    Answer: A road

11. What is something you will never see again?

    Answer: Yesterday

12. Jack rode into town on Friday and rode out two days later on Friday. How can that be possible?

    Answer: Friday is his horse's name

13. If two is company and three is a crowd, what are four and five?

    Answer: Nine

14. What is the center of Gravity?

    Answer: The letter V

15. A lawyer, a plumber, and a hat maker were walking down the street. Who had the biggest hat?

    Answer: The one with the biggest head

16. What kind of room has no doors or windows?

    Answer: A mushroom

17. How many seconds are there in a year?

    Answer: 12 – January 2nd, February 2nd, March 2nd, April 2nd . . .

18. Who is the fastest runner in the whole world?

    Answer: Adam. Because he was the first in the human race

19. What has a face and two hands but no arms or legs?

    Answer: A clock

20. What five-letter word becomes shorter when you add two letters to it?

    Answer: Short

21. What word begins and ends with an E but only has one letter?

    Answer: Envelope

22. What has a neck but no head?

    Answer: A bottle

23. What type of cheese is made backwards?

    Answer: Edam

24. What gets wetter as it dries?

    Answer: A towel

25. Why did the boy bury his flashlight?

    Answer: Because the batteries died

26. Which letter of the alphabet has the most water?

    Answer: C

27. What starts with a P, ends with an E and has thousands of letters?

    Answer: The Post Office

28. What has to be broken before you can use it?

    Answer: An egg

29. Why would a man living in New York not be buried in Chicago?

    Answer: Because he is still living

30. What begins with T ends with T and has T in it?

Answer: A teapot

31. How many letters are there in the English alphabet?

    Answer: There are 18: 3 in the, 7 in English, and 8 in alphabet.

32. Which month has 28 days?

    Answer: All of them, of course

33. Three men were in a boat. It capsized, but only two got their hair wet. Why?

    Answer: One was bald

34. If everyone bought a white car, what would we have?

    Answer: A white carnation

35. How many letters are there in the alphabet?

    Answer: Eleven – T-h-e A-l-p-h-a-b-e-t

36. Where does Friday come before Thursday?

    Answer: In the dictionary

37. What is the difference between a jeweler and a jailer?

    Answer: A jeweler sells watches. A jailer watches cells.

38. What ship has two mates, but no captain?

    Answer: A relationship

39. When is a door not a door?

    Answer: When it is a jar

40. Bobby throws a ball as hard as he can. It comes back to him, even though nothing and nobody touches it. How?

Answer: He throws it straight up.

41. Mary's father has five daughters – Nana, Nene, Nini, Nono. What is the fifth daughter's name?

Answer: If you answered Nunu, you are wrong. It is Mary!

42. What occurs once in a minute, twice in a moment, and never in one thousand years?

Answer: The letter M

43. What is so delicate that saying its name breaks it?

Answer: Silence

44. What kind of tree can you carry in your hand?

Answer: A palm

45. If an electric train is travelling south, which way is the smoke going?

Answer: There is no smoke; it is an electric train!

46. You draw a line. Without touching it, how do you make the line longer?

Answer: You draw a shorter line next to it, and then it becomes the longer line.

47. They come out at night without being called, and are lost in the day without being stolen. What are they?

Answer: Stars

48. What is next in this sequence? JFMAMJJASON . . .

Answer: The letter "D." The sequence contains the first letter of each month.

49. What can make an octopus laugh?

    Answer: Ten tickles (tentacles)

50. Why do lions eat raw meat?

    Answer: Because they never learned to cook

51. What do lazy dogs do for fun?

    Answer: Chase parked cars

52. Where do cows go for their holidays?

    Answer: Moo York

53. What goes up but never goes down?

    Answer: Your age

54. Why did Mickey Mouse become an astronaut?

    Answer: He wanted to visit Pluto.

55. Why do bees hum?

    Answer: Because they do not know the words

56. What is the last thing you take off before bed?

    Answer: Your feet off the floor

57. If you threw a White stone into the Red Sea, what would it become?

    Answer: Wet

58. What gets wetter and wetter the more it dries?

    Answer: A towel

59. What invention lets you look right through a wall?

    Answer: A window

60. What has four legs, but can't walk?

    Answer: A table

61. How do you make the number one disappear?

    Answer: Add the letter G and it's "gone"

62. A monkey, a squirrel, and a bird are racing to the top of a coconut tree. Who will get the banana first, the monkey, the squirrel, or the bird?

    Answer: None of them, because you cannot get a banana from a coconut tree!

63. Why is an island like the letter T?

    Answer: Because it is in the middle of water.

64. How can a pants pocket be empty and still have something in it?

    Answer: It can have a hole in it.

MEDIUM DIFFICULTY

1. Q: If four people can repair four bicycles in four hours, how many bicycles can eight people repair in eight hours?

    A: 16 bicycles.

2. Q: You walk into a room with a match, a kerosene lamp, a candle, and a fireplace. Which do you light first?

    A: The match.

3. Q: What word begins and ends with an E but only has one letter?

    A: Envelope.

4. Q: Railroad crossing, watch out for cars. Can you spell that without any Rs?

    A: T-H-A-T.

5. Q: A man was taking a walk outside when it started to rain. The man didn't have an umbrella, and he wasn't wearing a hat. His clothes got soaked, yet not a single hair on his head got wet. How could this happen?

    A: The man was bald.

6. Q: How many seconds are there in a year?

    A: Twelve. January 2nd, February 2nd, March 2nd...

7. Q: Name four days of the week that start with the letter "T."

    A: Tuesday, Thursday, today, and tomorrow.

8. Q: A boy was rushed to the hospital emergency room. The ER doctor saw the boy and said, "I cannot operate on this boy. He is my son." But the doctor was not the boy's father. How could that be?

   A: The doctor was his mom.

9. Q: What can run but can't walk?

   A: A drop of water.

10. Q: What's full of holes but still holds water?

    A: A sponge.

11. Q: What has one eye but can't see?

    A: A needle.

12. Q: What word looks the same backward and upside down?

    A: SWIMS.

13. Q: What does this mean? "I RIGHT I"

    A: Right between the eyes.

14. Q: A boy fell off a 20-foot ladder but did not get hurt. Why not?

    A: He fell off the bottom step.

15. Q: What five-letter word becomes shorter when you add two letters to it?

    A: Short.

16. Q: If you are running in a race and you pass the person in second place, what place are you in?

    A: Second place.

17. Q: How many letters are there in the alphabet?

    A: Eleven: T-H-E-A-L-P-H-A-B-E-T.

18. I am a word. If you pronounce me rightly, it will be wrong. If you pronounce me wrong it is right? What word am I?

Answer: Wrong

19. I don't have eyes, ears, nose and tongue, but I can see, smell, hear and taste everything. What am I?

Answer: A brain

20. I do not have wings, but I can fly. I don't have eyes, but I will cry! What am I?

Answer: A cloud

21. I do not speak, cannot hear or speak anything, but I will always tell the truth. What am I?

Answer: A mirror

22. I go around all the places, cities, towns and villages, but never come inside. What am I?

Answer: A street

23. I have lots of memories, but I own nothing. What am I?

Answer: A photo frame

24. I have no legs. I will never walk, but always run. What am I?

Answer: A river

25. I have no life, but I can die, what am I?

Answer: A battery

26. I have rivers, but do not have water. I have dense forests, but no trees and animals. I have cities, but no people live in those cities. What am I?

Answer: A map

27. I never ask questions, but always answered. What am I?

Answer: A doorbell

28. I was born big, but as the day passes, as I get older, I become small. What am I?

Answer: A candle

29. I will always come, never arrive today. What am I?

Answer: Tomorrow

30. I am full of keys, but I cannot open any door. What am I?

Answer: A piano

31. I'm the end of the colorful rainbow. What am I?

Answer: Water

32. I'm with poor people and rich people don't have me. If you eat me, you will die. What am I?

Answer: I am nothing.

33. If you give me water, I will die. What am I?

Answer: Fire

34. Many times you need me. The more and more you take me further, the more and more you leave me behind. What am I?

Answer: Footsteps

35. People buy me to eat, but never eat me. What am I?

Answer: A plate

36. The one who makes me does not need me, when he makes me. The one who buys me does not use

me for himself or herself. The one who uses me doesn't know that he or she is using me. What am I?

Answer: A coffin

37. When the water comes down, when it rains, I go up. What am I?

Answer: An umbrella

38. You can break me easily without even touching me or seeing me. What am I?

Answer: A promise

39. You will throw me away when you want to use me. You will take me in when you don't want to use me. What am I?

Answer: An anchor

40. I am tall when I am young and I am short when I am old. What am I?

    Answer: A candle

41. I have no bones and no legs, but if you keep me warm, I will soon walk away. What am I?

    Answer: An egg

42. If I drink, I die. If I eat, I am fine. What am I?

    Answer: A fire

43. Take away my first letter, and I still sound the same. Take away my last letter, I still sound the same. Even take away my letter in the middle, I will still sound the same. I am a five letter word. What am I?

    Answer: Empty

44. It is higher without the head, than with it. What is it?

    Answer: A pillow

45. The more it dries, the wetter it becomes. What is it?

    Answer: Water

46. Throw away the outside and cook the inside, then eat the outside and throw away the inside. What is it?

    Answer: Corn on the cob – because you throw away the husk, cook and eat the kernels, and throw away the cob.

47. It stands on one leg with its heart in its head. What is it?

    Answer: A cabbage

48. You can keep it only after giving it away to someone else. What is it?

    Answer: Your word

49. It has been around for millions of years, but it is no more than a month old. What is it?

    Answer: The moon

50. It lives without a body, hears without ears, speaks without a mouth, and is born in air. What is it?

    Answer: An echo

51. The more you take away, the larger it becomes? What is it?

    Answer: A hole

52. We see it once in a year, twice in a week, and never in a day. What is it?

    Answer: The letter "E"

53. If I have it, I do not share it. If I share it, I don't have it. What is it?

    Answer: A secret

54. Poor people have it. Rich people need it. If you eat it you die. What is it?

    Answer: Nothing

55. You can hear it, but not touch or see it. What is it?

    Answer: Your voice

56. It loses its head in the morning but gets it back at night? What is it?

    Answer: A pillow

57. It is round on both sides but high in the middle. What is it?

    Answer: Ohio.

58. It gets broken without being held. What is it?

Answer: A promise

59. It is always coming but never arrives? What is it?

Answer: Tomorrow

60. It has Eighty-eight keys but can't open a single door? What is it?

Answer: A piano

HARD DIFFICULTY

1. Q: How far can a dog run into the woods?

   A: The dog can run into the woods only halfway – if it ran any farther it would run out of the woods!

2. Q: My name is Ruger. I live on a farm. There are four other dogs on the farm with me. Their names are Snowy, Flash, Speedy, and Brownie. What do you think the fifth dog's name is?

   A: Ruger.

3. Q: Why do birds fly south for the winter?

   A: It's too far to walk.

4.   Q: How do dog catchers get paid?

A: By the pound.

5.   Q: What two keys can't open any door?

A: A monkey and a donkey.

6.   Q: A cowboy rides into town on Friday, stays for three days, then leaves on Friday. How did he do it?

A: His horse's name was Friday.

7.   Q: If three dogs and one cat weren't standing under an umbrella, how did none of them get wet?

A: It wasn't raining!

8.   Q: How many animals did Moses take on the ark?

A: Moses didn't take anything on the ark. Noah did.

9. Q: What do dogs have that no other animal has?

    A: Puppies.

10. Q: A dog is on a 10-foot chain but wants a bone that
    is 11 feet away. How can the dog get the bone?

    A: The chain isn't attached to anything.

11. Q: Why couldn't Goldilocks sleep?

    A: Because of night-bears.

12. Q: Why did the pony cough?

    A: He was a little horse.

13. Q: When is a man like a snake?

    A: When he's rattled.

14. Q: I travel very slowly when gliding along the ground. Maybe my shell weighs me down. In your garden, I am found. What am I?

A: A snail.

15. Q: What has two heads, four eyes, six legs, and a tail?

A: A cowboy riding his horse.

16. Q: I can jump and I can climb. With my many legs, I swing from tree to tree. I can build a house much bigger than me. What am I?

A: A spider.

17. Q: What kind of music do rabbits like?

A: Hip Hop.

18. Q: How did the chimp fix the leaky faucet?

A: With a Monkey Wrench.

19. Q: I have four legs but no tail. Usually, you can only hear me at night. What am I?

    A: A frog.

20. Q: What did the turkey say to the rooster when he challenged him to a fight?

    A: Are you a chicken?

21. Q: I am known as a king. The jungle is where I reign. It's hard to tame me. And I have a large mane. What am I?

    A: A lion.

22. There is a rooster sitting on top of a barn. If it laid an egg, which way would it roll?"

    Answer: Roosters don't lay eggs.

23. What five letter word becomes shorter when you add two letters to it?"

Answer: Short (short+er).

24. What is so fragile that saying its name breaks it?"

Answer: Silence.

25. What has a bottom at the top?"

Answer: Your legs.

26. What has a face and two hands but no arms or legs?"

Answer: A clock.

27. How many months have 28 days?"

Answer: All 12 of them do.

28. What's black and white and read all over?"

Answer: A newspaper.

29. What word is spelled wrong in every dictionary?"

Answer: Wrong.

30. I have no life, but I can die. What am I?"

Answer: A battery.

31. What gets wetter as it dries?"

Answer: A towel.

32. Mary has four daughters, and each of her daughters has a brother — how many children does Mary have?"

Answer: Five. Each daughter has the same single brother.

33. You walk into a room which contains a match, a kerosene lamp, a candle, and a fireplace. What would you light first?"

    Answer: The match.

34. What has four wheels and flies?"

    Answer: A garbage truck.

35. What has 88 keys, but cannot open a single door?"

    Answer: A piano.

36. What has a bed but never sleeps, can run but never walks, and has a bank but no money?"

    Answer: A river.

37. The more you take the more you leave behind. What are they?"

    Answer: Footsteps.

38. What is full of holes but still holds water?"

    Answer: A sponge.

39. Who can shave 25 times a day but still have a beard?"

    Answer: A barber.

40. What begins with T, finishes with T, and has "T" in it?"

    Answer: A teapot.

41. Which weighs more: a pound of feathers or a pound of bricks?"

    Answer: They weigh the same.

42. Everyone has it and no one can lose it; what is it?"

    Answer: A shadow.

43. What goes up but never goes back down?"

Answer: Your age.

44. What has one head, one foot, and four legs?"

Answer: A bed.

45. What begins with an E but only has one letter in it?"

Answer: An envelope.

46. I am an odd number. Take away a letter and I become even. What number am I?"

Answer: Seven.

47. After a train crashed, every single person died. Who survived?"

Answer: All of the couples.

48. What gets bigger the more you take away?"

    Answer: A hole.

49. What's bright orange with green on top and sounds
    like a parrot?

    Answer: A carrot

50. What's really easy to get into, and hard to get out
    of?

    Answer: Trouble

51. Break it and it gets better, Immediately set and
    harder to break again.

    Answer: Record

52. You cannot see me, nor can I be touched, you
    cannot feel me, but I can cook your lunch!

    Answer: A microwave particle

53. After booming and zapping is when I emerge, to bring you bright dazzling beauty when I diverge. Some say that I hide enormous wealth, but those riches have always proven stealth. What am I?

Answer: A rainbow

54. I am used in most sports, have four holes, come in many different colors and there is a state that shares my name. What am I?

Answer: A jersey

55. I am a fruit, I am a bird and I am also a person. What am I?

Answer: Kiwi

56. Q: The one who made it didn't want it. The one who bought it didn't need it. The one who used it never saw it. What is it?

A: A coffin.

57. Q: What needs an answer but doesn't ask a
question?

    A: A telephone.

58. Q: If I have it, I don't share it. If I share it, I don't
have it. What is it?

    A: A secret.

59. Q: Forward I am heavy, but backward I am not.
What am I?

    A: Ton.

60. Q: What is always late and never present now?

    A: Later.

61. Q: A cloud is my mother, the wind is my father, my
son is the cool stream, and my daughter is the fruit

of the land. A rainbow is my bed, the earth my final resting place, and I am the torment of man.

A: Rain

62. Q: What belongs to you but others use it more than you do?

A: Your name

63. Q: I am taken from a mine and shut up in a wooden case, from which I am never released, and yet I am used by almost everybody. What am I?

A: Pencil lead

64. Q: What goes up the chimney when down, but cannot go down the chimney when up?

A: An umbrella

HARDEST DIFFICULTY

1. Add the number to the number itself and then multiply by 4. Again divide the number by 8 and you will get the same number once more. Which is that number?

   Answer: Any number

2. At the time of shipping, Tom can place 10 small boxes or 8 large boxes into a carton. A total of 96 boxes were sent in one shipment. The number of small boxes was less than large boxes. What is the total number of cartons he shipped?

   Answer: 11 cartons

   4 small boxes (4*10 = 40 boxes)

   7 large boxes (7*8 = 56 boxes)

   So 96 boxes and 11 total cartons

3. X is an odd number. Take an alphabet away from X and it becomes even. Which is that number?

   Answer: Seven (Seven-S=Even)

4. You are given 3 positive numbers. You can add these numbers and multiply them together. The result you get will be the same. Which are the numbers?

   Answer: 1, 2 and 3

5. I have a barrel of wine and your job is to measure out one gallon from it. I can give you a five-gallon container and three-gallon container? How can you help me?

   Answer: First of all fill up the 3 gallon container with wine. After that you have to transfer the same to the 5 gallon container. Then fill up the 3 gallon container again and transfer the wine to the 5 gallon container until it is full. The left over in the 3-gallon container is 1 gallon of wine.

6. Tom was asked to paint the number plates on 100 apartments which means he will have to paint numbers 1 through 100. Can you figure out the number of times he will have to paint the number 8?

Answer: 20 times. (8, 18, 28, 38, 48, 58, 68, 78, 80, 81, 82, 83, 84, 85, 86, 87, 88, 89, 98)

7. What is the maximum possible number of times you can subtract number 5 from number 25?

Answer: Only once. This is because when you subtract 5 from 25 for the first time, it becomes number 20, then 15 and so on.

8. William has a toaster with 2 slots. So he can toast one side each of 2 breads simultaneously which takes 1 minute. He wanted to make 3 pieces of toast for his breakfast. What is the minimum time required to do so?

Answer: 3 minutes! First of all, he can put two pieces of bread in the toaster. After 1 minute, one side each of the 2 breads get toasted. He can then flip a side of bread and take the other one out. And he can place the 3rd piece of bread into the free space of the toaster. After the second minute, he can take the completely toasted bread out and flip the other one. Then place the half toasted bread into the free space to toast the fresh side. After 3 minutes, all 3 pieces of breads gets toasted.

9. I am a three digit number. My second digit is 4 times bigger than the third digit. My first digit is 3 less than my second digit. Who am I?

Answer: 141

10. You are given a telephone and asked to multiply all the numbers on the device's number pad. What will be the answer?

Answer: zero (The number pad contains number 0. When you multiply any number by zero, the answer will be zero)

11. Raj has 2 books. One of the books is faced upside-down and the second book is rotated which makes the top of the book facing Raj. Then what will be the total sum of the 1st pages in each of these books?

Answer: 2. Regardless of how the books are oriented, the first page of every book is page number 1. So 1 + 1 = 2!

12. I have a pound of feathers and a pound of iron? Can you please tell me which one weighs more?

Answer: Both of them would be of same weight. A pound remains a pound despite the type of object.

13. A mobile phone and its case cost Rs. 110 in total. The price of the mobile phone is Rs.100 more than its case. What is the price of the mobile phone?

Answer: Rs.105 (not Rs.110)

14. 100 coins fell down and got scattered inside a dark place. 90 of the coins fell with heads facing up and the rest 10 coins fell with tails up. You are asked to sort out these coins into 2 piles. However, each pile should have the same count of tails up coins. How is it possible?

Answer: First of all the piles need not be of the same size. I can make 2 piles, one with 90 coins and the other with 10 coins. Now I just flip all of the 10 coins on the pile. So the piles will have the same count of tails.

15. Robin tosses a coin 10 times and it landed in the heads up position all ten times. So what are the possible chances for him to toss it up again and gets landed in heads up position?

Answer: He has a 50 percent chance to toss the coin and see the heads up position. This is because the coin toss is not dependent on the first 10 tosses.

16. There are 100 pairs of dogs in a zoo. Two pairs of babies are born for every dog. Unfortunately, 23 of the dogs have not survived. How many dogs would be left in total?

    Answer: 977 dogs (100 x 2 = 200; 200 + 800 = 1000; 1000 − 23 = 977)

17. If you multiply me by any other number, the answer will always remain the same. Who am I?

    Answer: zero

18. The price of a duck is Rs. 9, a spider costs Rs. 36 and a bee was priced Rs. 27. By taking into account this information, what will be the price of a cat?

    Answer: Rs.18 (Rs. 4.50 per leg)

19. It takes 12 men 12 hours to construct a wall. Then how long will it take for 6 men to complete the same wall?

    Answer: No time! There is no need of constructing

it again as the job is already done.

20. There are 6 black socks, 8 brown socks, 4 blue socks, and 2 red socks in my sock drawer. Can you figure out the minimum number of socks to be pulled out in order to get a matching pair for sure?

    Answer: At least 5

21. 1/2 of 2/3 of 3/4 of 4/5 of 5/6 of 6/7 of 7/8 of 8/9 of 9/10 of 10,000. Can you solve this in a single step?

    Answer: 1000! 1/10 of 10,000 give 1000. (Everything gets cancel out if you multiply all of these fractions and the remaining will be 1/10)

22. A man is twice as old as his little sister. He is also half as old as their dad. Over a period of 50 years, the age of the sister will become half of their dad's age. What is the age of the man now?

    Answer: He is 50 years old.

23. Tom and Peter live in different parts of city but studies in the same high school. Tom left for school 10 minutes before Peter started and they happened to meet at a park. At the time of their meeting, who was closer to the school?

Answer: They are both at the same distance from school as they met in the same place.

24. You are given a sequence: 1 11 21 1211 111221 312211. Can you figure out the next number in this sequence?

Answer: 13112221 (Each of the number in the sequence is the description of the previous number. If you start with 1, the 2nd number is 11 (one 1), third number is 21 (two 1's), fourth number is 1211 (one 2, one 1) and so on.

25. Seven boys met each other in a party. Each of them shakes hands only once with each of the other

boys. What is the total number of handshakes that took place?

Answer: Twenty one

26. Amir has 2 buckets with him. The first bucket had only red marbles and the other one had only brown marbles. The 2 of these buckets has equal number of marbles. What type of arrangement can he make to increase the possibility of grabbing a red marble from each of the buckets?

Answer: Keep only a single red marble in one bucket and the remaining red and brown marbles in the other bucket. This increases his chances of grabbing a red marble from each of the bucket (75% approx) which is not possible with any other arrangement.

27. Ravi has two kids. If the elder kid is a boy, then what is the possibility that his other kid is also a boy?

Answer: 50 percent

28. A group of students were standing in the blazing sun facing due west on a march past event. The leader shouted at them: Right turn! About turn! Left turn! At the end of these commands, in which direction is the students facing now?

Answer: East. They will turn 90 degrees in a right turn, and they turn180 degrees in an about turn, and finally they turn 90 degrees in a left turn. Therefore, the students are now facing east.

29. Tom was on the way to KLCC Park. He met a guy with 7 wives and each of them came with 7 sacks. All these sacks contain 7 cats and each of these 7 cats had 7 kits. So in total, how many were going to KLCC Park?

Answer: 1. Only Tom was going to KLCC Park.

30. There are a certain number of books on my bookshelf. I took a book which is 6th from the right

and 4th from the left. Can you find out the number of books on my shelf?

Answer: 9 ((6+4)-1. Or you just arrange a set of 10 books and see how it works)

31. A grandfather, two fathers and two sons drove to park together. Each of them bought one entry ticket each. How many tickets have they bought in total?

Answer: 3 (there were only 3 people as the father is also a son and grandfather is also a father)

32. Two aeroplanes started the voyage. One flight is flying from London to KL at a speed of 400 MPH. The other flight is flying from KL to London at a speed of 600 MPH. Both these flights met at a point. Which of these flights will be closer to KL?

Answer: Both these flights will be at the same distance from KL when they meet.

33. 5+5+5=550. You can draw just a single straight line to make this equation true. How is it possible?

Answer: You can draw a straight line on the first plus sign. This makes it number 4. Now the equation looks like 545+5=550 which is true. Or you can simply draw a cross line on the equal symbol to make it "not equal to".

Also Read: 13 Puzzles to Boost Students Logical Thinking

34. Tom weighs half as much as Peter and Jerry weigh 3 times the weight of Tom. Their total weight is 720 pounds. Can you figure out the individual weights of each man?

Answer: Peter weighs twice the weight of Tom, and Jerry weighs three times of the same. So you can divide their total weight by 6 to get Tom's weight

$X + 2x + 3x = 720$

By dividing 720 by 6, we can understand that Tom weighs 120 Pounds. Considering this value, Peter weighs 240 Pounds and Jerry weighs 360 Pounds.

35. Mary has 7 daughters and each of them has a brother. Can you figure out the total number of kids Mary have?

    Answer: 8 kids because the sisters have just one brother in common.

36. There is an empty basket that is one foot in diameter. Can you tell the total number of eggs that you can put in this empty basket?

    Answer: Only One Egg! Once you put an egg into the basket, it doesn't remain empty anymore.

37. When my dad was 31 years old, I was just 8 years. Now his age is twice as old as my age. What is my present age?

    Answer: When you calculate the difference between the ages, you can see that it is 23 years. So you must be 23 years old now.

38. There is a golf club that is formed for men only. The club comprises a total of 600. 5% of the total men in the club have one tattoo. By taking into account the other 95% members, half of them have two tattoos and the remaining men have no tattoos. What is the total number of tattoos that you can see in the club?

Answer: 600. According to the information 5% or 30 of them are having one tattoo. Among the other 95% or 570 men, half of them have two tattoos and the rest half have none. This is equivalent to all of them having a tattoo.

39. 27 hens were marching towards the farm. 5 of them lost their way, 13 hens returned, and 9 hens finally reached the farm. What happened to the remaining hens?

Answer: None of the hens are remaining now! (27-5= 22; 22-13= 9, 9-9=0)

40. 1=3, 2=3, 3=5, 4=4, 5=4, 6=3, 7=5, 8=5, 9=4, 10=3, 11=? 12=? Can you complete the sequence?

    Answer: 6! The numbers indicate the number of letters in the spelling of the corresponding number.

41. X is a three digit number. The tens digit is 5 more than the ones digit. The hundreds digit is 8 less than the tens digit. What is X?

    Answer: Number 194.

42. 100 girls were attending a party. 85 of them had a red bag, 75 of them have worn brown shoes, 60 of them came with an umbrella and 90 girls wore a ring. How many girls have had all these four items?

    Answer: 10

    Divide by 3. All the girls had three items. The remainder indicates the number of girls with 4 items.

    85

    75

60

90

------

3 = 100 + 10 remainder

43. When you add eight 8's, the result you get will be number 1,000. How is it possible? You are permitted to use only addition to solve the problem.

Answer: 888 + 88 + 8 + 8 + 8 = 1,000

44. Thomas saw some cigarette butts on the ground on his way home. He thought to make cigarettes with these buds and 4 butts makes one cigarette. There were 16 cigarette butts on the ground. What is the maximum possible number of cigarettes he can make out of them?

Answer: 5. First he can make 4 cigarettes with those 16 butts. When he smokes those 4 cigarettes, he will get 4 more butts and he can make one more cigarette with it.

45. Ravi had two ropes with him and both these ropes need exactly 1 hour in order to get burnt from 1 end to the other end. There is no option to cut the rope. So what is the possibility that he can burn the 2 ropes in just 45 minutes?solve this

    Answer: Light up both sides of the first rope with fire so that it starts burning from both ends and fire up the second rope on one side only. In half an hour, the first rope will get completely burnt and the second rope will be burnt only half. At this particular time, you have to light up the second rope from the other side. So rest of the rope gets burnt in 15 minutes. This makes it a total of 45 minutes for two ropes to burn entirely.

46. Suppose 1+9+8=1, then what can be 2+8+9?

    Answer: 10! (Consider the first letter of the spelling of each digit, One+Nine+Eight= ONE, similarly Two+Eight+Nine= TEN)

47. Two hens can lay two eggs in two minutes. If this is the maximum speed possible, what is the total number of hen needed to get 500 eggs in 500 minutes?

    Answer: 2 hens

48. Sam was born on January 1st, 23 B.C. in KL town and passed away on January 2nd, 23 A.D. What was his age when he died?

    Answer: 45 years old! There are 23 years in both periods in actual calculation but there is no 0 year. So you can add up these periods and subtract 1 year. That means $23 + 23 - 1 = 45$ years old.

49. Peter was asked how old he was. His reply was like this "In a period of 2 years my age will be twice my age when you asked this five years ago" How old is he?

    Answer: Let Peter's age be X Years

    X+2=2(X-5)

    X+2=2X-10

X=12

50. What is inanimate, yet can stand up,

Can start out copper and end up as steel,

So fragile, a child could break one,

But many have the strength to lift a man?

What is it?

Answer: A human hair

51. Looks like water,

But it's heat.

Sits on sand,

Lays on concrete.

People have been known,

To follow it everywhere.

But it gets them no place,

And all they can do is stare.

Answer: A mirage

52. I have three feet, but I can't stand without leaning.

    To make matters worse I have no arms to lean with.

    Please be good so that I'm not called into use.

    What am I?

    Answer: A Yardstick

53. I breath and things get hot,

    though my heart is light as wind.

    The swordsman knows me not,

    though I helped to make his friend.

    I cannot do my job alone,

    Though others make me sigh,

    By their strength my job is done,

    So tell me, what am I?

    Answer: Bellows

54. I'm not really more than holes tied to more holes;

    I'm strong as good steel, though not as stiff as a pole.

    Answer: Chain

55. Pronounced as one letter, And written with three, Two letters there are, And two only in me. I'm double, I'm single, I'm black blue and grey, I'm read from both ends, And the same either way.

    Answer: Eye

56. They can be harbored, but few hold water. You can nurse them, but only by holding them against someone else. You can carry them, but not with your arms. You can bury them, but not in the earth.

    Answer: Grudge

57. I have three syllables. Take away five letters, a male will remain. Take away four letters, a female will remain. Take away three letters, a great man will appear. The entire word shows you what Joan of Arc was.

    Answer: Heroine

58. I was trapped in a jail cell.

All I had was a mirror and a wooden table.

How did I escape? (Hint: The answer only makes sense if you say it aloud.)

Answer: I looked in the mirror and saw what I saw. I took the saw and cut the table in half. Two halves make a whole. I escaped through the hole.

59. What word has kst in the middle, in the beginning, and at the end?

Answer: Inkstand

60. Curtail me thrice, I am a youth;

Behead me once, a snake;

Complete, I'm often used, in truth,

When certain steps you'd take.

What Am I?

Answer: Ladder

CONCLUSION

Wow! You made it through all 300 of the mind twisting riddles and challenging brain teasers in this book.... How did they go? Did you have fun? These riddles have all been hand picked in order to challenge your brain and entertain the heck out of you! We hope you enjoyed going through them and they created some great memories between you, your friends and your family.

Once again, we would like to thank you for reading our book *Riddles and Brain Teasers for Smart Kids* and we can't wait to hear what you thought about it. If you enjoyed listening to this book, please don't forget to leave a review and let us know exactly how much you loved it. Reviews mean the world to us and help us continue to create books just like this one for years to come.

Thank you!

DL Digital Entertainment

Made in the USA
Middletown, DE
21 March 2020